MA

An Inspiring Sport Story for Kids- The Dragon's Journey in Table Tennis, From Olympic Gold to Grand Slam Glory

Dale J. Gibson

Copyright

© 2025 by Dale J. Gibson. All rights reserved.

No part of this publication may be reproduced, distributed, or transmitted in any form or by any means, including photocopying, recording, or other electronic or mechanical methods, without the prior written permission of the publisher, except for the use of brief quotations in a review. The information contained in this book is intended solely for general educational use. The author has done his or her best to check the accuracy and reliability of the information within this book, but websites change frequently without notification.

Disclaimer

This book is an independently written and published biography for young readers, created to inspire and educate. It is not authorized, sponsored, or endorsed by the individual, team, organization, or any other official entity mentioned within.

Every effort has been made to ensure the accuracy of the information presented, based on publicly available sources. However, details such as dates, statistics, and events may be subject to change over time. This book is intended for educational and entertainment purposes only and should not be considered an official record.

Table of Contents

Introduction 1

Chapter 1 3

A Boy with a Dream 3

Chapter 2 8

Rising Through the Ranks 8

Chapter 3 13

The Champion's Mindset 13

Chapter 4 18

Conquering the World 18

Chapter 5 23

Olympic Glory 23

Chapter 6 28

The Grand Slam Winner 28

Chapter 7 32

A Leader on the Team 32

Chapter 8 36

Challenges and Comebacks 36

Chapter 9 40

More Than a Champion 40

Chapter 10 44

The Legend Lives On 44

Fun Facts, Glossary and Fun Quiz 48

Introduction

Have you ever seen a table tennis player move so fast that the ball seems to vanish? If you have, chances are you were watching Ma Long in action. Known as "The Dragon," he is not just a champion—he is a legend. His powerful smashes, pinpoint accuracy, and lightning-quick reflexes have made him one of the greatest table tennis players in history.

But Ma Long's story is not just about talent. It's about hard work, discipline, and never giving up. He wasn't born with a gold medal around his neck. Like every champion, he started small—just a boy with a paddle in his hand and a dream in his heart. While other kids were playing, Ma Long was training. While others rested, he kept pushing himself to be better. His journey to greatness was filled with challenges, but he never backed down.

From his early days in China to standing on the world's biggest stages, Ma Long has inspired millions with his determination and humility. He has won Olympic gold medals, World Championships, and even the rarest achievement in table tennis—the Grand Slam. But beyond the trophies and records, he remains a leader, a mentor, and a role model for young athletes around the world.

This book will take you on an exciting journey through Ma Long's life—from his first steps in the sport to his greatest victories. You will discover the dedication, sacrifices, and mindset that turned him into a true legend. Whether you are a table tennis fan or someone chasing a dream, Ma Long's story will inspire you to work hard and believe in yourself.

Are you ready to meet the Dragon? Let's begin!

Chapter 1

A Boy with a Dream

A Love for Table Tennis

Ma Long was born on October 20, 1988, in Anshan, a city in China known for its steel industry. But for young Ma Long, the most important thing wasn't steel—it was table tennis.

From the time he could walk, Ma Long was full of energy. He loved running, jumping, and playing games with the neighborhood kids. But one day, when he was five years old, something changed. His father brought home a small table tennis paddle and a plastic ball. At first, it was just a fun game. He would hit the ball against the wall, watching it bounce back toward him. Each time he missed, he tried again, determined to get better.

His father, Ma Yujun, noticed his son's excitement. "Do you like table tennis?" he asked one evening.

Ma Long nodded, his eyes shining. "Yes! It's so much fun!"

Seeing his son's enthusiasm, Ma Yujun decided to take him to a local sports center. It was a small place, but inside, the sound of paddles hitting balls filled the air. The moment Ma Long stepped in, he was fascinated. Older kids played fast matches, their movements quick and smooth. He watched in amazement, his heart pounding with excitement.

A coach named Wang Hongwei noticed Ma Long watching. "Would you like to try?" he asked.

Ma Long eagerly nodded, gripping his paddle tightly. He was shorter than the table, but that didn't stop him. When the first ball came his way, he swung with all his might—missing completely. But instead of getting discouraged, he laughed. "I'll get the next one!"

And he did. Slowly, he learned how to hit the ball, how to move his feet, and how to keep his eyes on the game. Even at such a young age, his determination was clear.

After that day, Ma Long begged his parents to take him back to the sports center. Every evening, while other kids were watching cartoons, he was practicing. He didn't know it yet, but this was the beginning of a journey that would change his life.

Training Hard from a Young Age

By the time Ma Long turned seven, he had already spent countless hours practicing table tennis. His parents saw his passion and decided to enroll him in a proper training program. He joined a local club where the training was much tougher.

Every morning before school, Ma Long would wake up early to practice his footwork. After school, while his friends played outside, he went straight to the training hall. There, he practiced for hours, hitting the ball over and over again until his arms felt heavy.

His coach was strict, often making him repeat drills hundreds of times. "Again!" the coach would shout whenever Ma Long made a mistake. Some days, his legs ached from moving so much, and his hands felt sore from gripping the paddle. But he never complained. He knew that to become great, he had to work harder than anyone else.

One evening, after a long day of practice, Ma Long's father found him hitting the ball against the wall in their home. "You should rest," his father said gently.

"I can't," Ma Long replied, shaking his head. "I have to get better."

His father smiled, proud of his son's determination. "Then keep going," he said.

By the time Ma Long was nine, his hard work was paying off. He started winning local tournaments, defeating players older and bigger than him. People began to notice the little boy with the serious expression and fast hands. Coaches started calling him a "child prodigy," a future star of Chinese table tennis.

But Ma Long knew he still had a long way to go.

Joining the National Team

When Ma Long turned eleven, he received the biggest opportunity of his young life—an invitation to train with the Liaoning Provincial Team. This was a huge step. The team was known for producing top players, and only the best young athletes were chosen.

Leaving home was not easy. His mother packed his bags with care, reminding him to eat well and take care of himself. His father gave him a pat on the shoulder. "Work hard, and don't give up," he said.

Ma Long nodded. He was nervous, but he was also excited. He knew that this was his chance to prove himself.

Training with the Liaoning team was much harder than anything he had experienced before. The coaches pushed him to his limits. He trained from morning until night, practicing drills, improving his speed, and sharpening his reflexes. Some days, he felt like he couldn't move another step. But then he would remind himself why he was there—to become the best.

At first, he struggled to keep up with the older players. They were stronger, faster, and more experienced. But Ma Long never let that discourage him. He listened to his coaches, learned from his mistakes, and kept practicing.

By the time he was thirteen, he had become one of the top young players in China. His performances caught the attention of the Chinese National

Team, the most elite table tennis team in the world. At just fifteen years old, Ma Long was invited to join the national squad, an achievement that few players ever reach.

Standing in the training hall of the national team for the first time, Ma Long took a deep breath. He had worked so hard to get there, but he knew this was just the beginning. The real challenge was about to begin.

Chapter 2

Rising Through the Ranks

Competing with the Best

By the time Ma Long joined the Chinese National Team at just 15 years old, he knew he had stepped into a whole new world. The training halls were bigger, the coaches stricter, and most importantly, the players were far stronger than anyone he had faced before.

Every day, he practiced alongside some of the best table tennis players in China. Many of them were older and more experienced, with years of high-level competition behind them. The speed of the game was faster than anything Ma Long had ever seen. The balls zipped across the table like tiny white rockets, and the rallies were fierce.

At first, Ma Long struggled to keep up. He lost matches during practice and often found himself outplayed by the senior players. But instead of getting frustrated, he paid close attention to everything around him. He watched how the older players positioned their feet, how they controlled the ball, and how they handled pressure. He knew that if he wanted to be the best, he had to learn from the best.

One of the players who inspired him the most was **Wang Liqin**, a Chinese superstar who had already won multiple world titles. Wang was strong, fast, and smart—everything a champion needed to be. Ma Long admired the way he played with confidence and precision. He made up his mind that one day, he would reach that level too.

Coach Liu Guoliang, a former Olympic champion himself, saw potential in Ma Long. "You have talent," he told the young player one day after practice. "But talent alone won't make you a champion. You need to work harder than everyone else."

Ma Long took those words to heart. He practiced longer hours, focused on improving his weaknesses, and never let a day go by without pushing himself. Slowly but surely, he started winning more practice matches. His movements became quicker, his shots sharper. The older players began to respect him—not just as a promising young talent, but as a serious competitor.

Learning from Defeats

With his hard work paying off, Ma Long started competing in international tournaments. In 2006, at just 17 years old, he played in the World Junior Championships and dominated the competition. He won the singles title, proving that he was one of the best young players in the world. But winning at the junior level was only the first step. The real challenge was competing with the top players in the men's division.

In 2007, Ma Long made his debut in the ITTF World Tour, a series of major table tennis tournaments featuring the best players from around the world. He faced off against stronger, more experienced opponents who had been playing at the highest level for years. The pressure was intense, and the matches were tough.

One of the most difficult moments of his early career came when he played against Ma Lin, an Olympic gold medalist and one of China's finest players. Ma Lin had a unique style—his unpredictable spins and quick attacks made it hard for opponents to find a rhythm. Ma Long gave everything he had in the match, but in the end, he lost.

Defeat was painful, but Ma Long didn't let it crush his spirit. Instead, he went back to the training hall and studied what had gone wrong. He practiced harder, focusing on improving his footwork and response to tricky spins. He knew that every loss was a lesson, and he was determined to learn.

Over the next couple of years, Ma Long continued to climb the ranks. He faced setbacks, losing important matches to world-class players like Timo Boll from Germany and Wang Hao from China. Each loss stung, but instead of feeling discouraged, he used them as motivation.

One night, after a particularly tough defeat, Ma Long sat alone in the training hall, bouncing a ball on his paddle. He thought about all the matches he had lost, all the points he had missed. But then, he reminded himself why he started playing table tennis in the first place.

"I won't give up," he whispered to himself. "I'll come back stronger."

First Big Wins

Ma Long's persistence paid off. In 2009, he made history by winning his first major ITTF World Cup title. He defeated some of the best players in the world, proving that he was no longer just a young talent—he was a real contender for the top spot.

That same year, he also helped China win gold at the World Table Tennis Championships in the team event. Playing alongside legends like Wang Hao and Ma Lin, he showed that he could handle high-pressure matches on the biggest stage. His confidence grew, and so did his skill level.

In 2010, Ma Long won his first China Open, a tournament that had always been special to him. Winning in front of his home crowd was a dream come true. The fans cheered his name as he raised the trophy high above his head. It was a moment he would never forget.

By 2011, Ma Long had climbed to the world number one ranking for the first time in his career. It was an incredible achievement, but he knew the journey was far from over. Staying at the top was just as hard as getting there.

He continued to push himself, training harder than ever. Every day, he reminded himself of his childhood dream—to be the best table tennis player in the world. And with every victory, that dream was coming true.

Chapter 3

The Champion's Mindset

Staying Focused Under Pressure

By the time Ma Long became one of the top table tennis players in the world, he had learned something important—champions aren't just made in training halls. They are made in moments of pressure.

Winning a match when everything is going well is easy. But what happens when the crowd is loud, the score is close, and your opponent is playing their best? That is when true champions are tested.

One of the biggest tests of Ma Long's career came in 2015 during the World Table Tennis Championships in Suzhou, China. He had made it to the finals, a step away from achieving his lifelong dream of becoming a world champion. His opponent was Fang Bo, another skilled Chinese player.

The crowd inside the stadium was electric. Fans waved Chinese flags and cheered loudly. Millions of people were watching from home. Ma Long felt the pressure building, but he took a deep breath and reminded himself, *One point at a time. Stay calm.*

The match began, and it was intense. Both players fought hard, trading powerful shots back and forth. Ma Long took the first game, but Fang Bo came back strong, winning the next two. Suddenly, Ma Long found himself trailing 1-2 in games. If he lost one more, his dream of becoming a world champion would be over.

This was the kind of moment that could break a player's confidence. But Ma Long refused to panic. He blocked out the noise, ignored the pressure, and focused only on the ball. He adjusted his strategy, attacking more aggressively and using his powerful forehand to take control of the game.

Point by point, he fought back. He won the fourth game, then the fifth. In the final game, he played with incredible speed and precision, leaving Fang Bo struggling to keep up. When Ma Long finally smashed the last ball past his opponent, the stadium erupted in cheers.

He had done it. Ma Long was the world champion!

As he raised the trophy above his head, he knew this victory was about more than just skill. It was about staying focused when it mattered most.

Never Giving Up

Even though Ma Long was now a world champion, his journey wasn't always smooth. In sports, as in life, setbacks are unavoidable. What matters is how you respond.

In 2016, Ma Long set his sights on the biggest prize of all—the Olympic gold medal. The Olympics only happen once every four years, and for a Chinese table tennis player, winning gold is the highest honor.

But there was a big obstacle in his way—Zhang Jike, another Chinese superstar. Zhang was known for his incredible backhand and fierce competitive spirit. He had already won Olympic gold in 2012, and he was determined to defend his title.

The two faced off in the men's singles final at the 2016 Rio Olympics. It was a dream match, with the two best players in the world battling for the gold.

The first game started, and Ma Long immediately took control. He played fast and smart, using his forehand to dominate the rallies. He won the first two games, but Zhang Jike wasn't ready to give up. In the third game, Zhang fought back, taking it with a series of brilliant shots.

For a brief moment, doubt crept into Ma Long's mind. What if Zhang Jike turned the match around? What if he lost after coming so close?

But then he reminded himself of all the times he had fought through tough moments before. He had spent years preparing for this. He would not give up now.

With renewed determination, he stepped back to the table. He played his best table tennis yet, winning the next two games to claim victory. Ma Long was now an Olympic champion!

Tears welled up in his eyes as he stood on the podium, the Chinese flag rising behind him. He had reached the top, but more importantly, he had proved to himself—and to the world—that he would never give up.

The Importance of Hard Work

Many people look at Ma Long's success and think, *He must have been born talented*. But talent alone is never enough. Behind every trophy, every title, and every victory was years of hard work.

Ma Long's training routine was intense. He spent six to eight hours a day practicing, repeating the same drills over and over until they became second nature. He worked on his footwork, speed, and accuracy, making sure every movement was perfect.

But it wasn't just about physical training. He also trained his mind. Table tennis is a game of speed and strategy. A player must think quickly, react instantly, and stay one step ahead of their opponent.

To improve his focus, Ma Long did mental exercises. He practiced controlling his breathing, staying calm under pressure, and blocking out distractions. He visualized matches in his mind, imagining different strategies and ways to win.

His hard work paid off. In 2017, he led China to victory in the World Table Tennis Championships again. In 2019, he became the first male player in history to win three consecutive World Championships—a record that cemented his place as one of the greatest players of all time.

Even after achieving so much, Ma Long never stopped working hard. When younger players like Fan Zhendong started challenging him, he trained even harder to stay ahead. He understood that true champions never stop improving.

One day, a young player asked him, "What is the secret to becoming a great table tennis player?"

Ma Long smiled and said, "There is no secret. You just have to love the game and work harder than everyone else."

And that is the mindset that made Ma Long a champion.

Chapter 4

Conquering the World

Winning His First World Championship

By 2015, Ma Long had already won many tournaments, broken records, and even held the world number one ranking for years. But there was one title missing from his collection—the World Table Tennis Championships singles title.

For years, Ma Long had come close but never won. The tournament, held every two years, was the most prestigious event in table tennis. Only the very best could win it, and China had many great players competing for the same prize.

In 2011, Ma Long was one of the favorites to win, but he lost in the semifinals to his teammate Wang Hao. Then, in 2013, he suffered another heartbreaking loss, this time to Zhang Jike, who went on to win the title. Each defeat was painful, but Ma Long refused to give up. He trained even harder, determined to take the trophy the next time.

Finally, in 2015, the World Championships were held in Suzhou, China. Ma Long was at his peak, playing better than ever. He had spent years preparing for this moment, and he wasn't going to let it slip away again.

Match by match, he fought his way through the tournament. In the quarterfinals, he faced Fan Zhendong, a rising young star who was being called the "future of Chinese table tennis." Fan was fast, powerful, and fearless, but Ma Long used his experience and strategy to win the match.

In the semifinals, he went up against Zhang Jike, the very player who had defeated him in 2013. This time, Ma Long was ready. He played aggressively, not giving Zhang any chance to attack. The match ended in Ma Long's favor, and he finally advanced to the final.

His opponent in the final was Fang Bo, another Chinese player who had surprised everyone by making it this far. Fang played incredibly well, winning two games and putting Ma Long in a tough position. But Ma Long stayed calm, focused on his game, and fought back. With powerful forehand attacks and precise backhand blocks, he turned the match around and won.

The moment he scored the final point, he dropped to his knees in relief and joy. He was finally the world champion!

As he lifted the trophy, tears filled his eyes. Years of hard work, failures, and determination had led to this moment. He had proven to himself and the world that he was the best.

Facing Tough Opponents

Winning the World Championships was a huge achievement, but Ma Long knew that staying on top would be even harder. There were many great players who wanted to take his spot.

One of his biggest rivals was Fan Zhendong. Fan was younger, stronger, and eager to become the best. Every time they played, the matches were intense, with powerful rallies and lightning-fast reactions. Ma Long had to use all his experience to outplay him.

Another tough opponent was Xu Xin, a left-handed player with incredible skill in spinning the ball. Xu's unique playing style made it difficult for anyone to predict his shots. But Ma Long studied his game carefully, found weaknesses, and learned how to counter his tricky spins.

International players like Timo Boll from Germany and Dimitrij Ovtcharov from Germany also pushed Ma Long to his limits. Boll, a veteran player, had a smart and strategic way of playing, while Ovtcharov had powerful shots and quick movements.

But no matter how tough his opponents were, Ma Long never backed down. He analyzed their styles, trained harder, and made sure he was always improving.

Becoming the Best

By 2016, Ma Long had won almost every major title in table tennis. But there was one last goal left—winning Olympic gold.

The 2016 Rio Olympics was his chance to make history. He had already won the World Championships, the World Cup, and held the world number one ranking. If he won gold, he would become the first player in history to hold all three major titles at the same time.

His biggest challenge came in the Olympic final, where he faced Zhang Jike, the defending champion. The world was watching as the two best players battled for gold.

Ma Long played with incredible confidence. He dominated the match, winning in straight games 4-0. His forehand was unstoppable, his backhand precise, and his footwork flawless.

As the final ball bounced off Zhang Jike's paddle and out, Ma Long threw his arms in the air. He was an Olympic champion!

Standing on the podium, with the Chinese flag rising behind him and the gold medal around his neck, Ma Long felt a deep sense of pride. He had achieved his dream. He was officially the best table tennis player in the world.

But even after conquering the world, Ma Long knew that his journey wasn't over. True champions don't stop at one victory—they keep pushing themselves, always striving for more.

And that's exactly what Ma Long did.

Chapter 5

Olympic Glory

Road to the Olympics

For any athlete, the Olympics is the biggest stage in the world. It is where the greatest players from every country compete for the ultimate prize—a gold medal.

For Ma Long, the dream of becoming an Olympic champion started when he was a young boy watching the 2004 Athens Olympics. That year, China's Wang Hao reached the men's singles final but lost to Ryu Seung-min of South Korea. Ma Long was just 16 years old at the time, but he promised himself that one day, he would bring home gold for China.

By the time the 2012 London Olympics came around, Ma Long was one of the top players in the world. However, China had a strict selection process, and only two players from each country could compete in the singles event. That year, the spots went to Zhang Jike and Wang Hao, leaving Ma Long out of the singles competition.

Although he played in the team event and helped China win gold, missing out on the singles event was heartbreaking. He had trained so hard, but he didn't even get the chance to compete for an individual medal. However, instead of feeling sorry for himself, Ma Long used the disappointment as motivation.

"If I don't want to feel this way again," he told himself, "I have to work harder than ever before."

For the next four years, he trained with even greater determination. He worked on his weaknesses, improved his speed, and strengthened his mental game. He knew that if he wanted to become an Olympic champion, he had to be the best in the world.

By the time the 2016 Rio Olympics arrived, Ma Long had proven himself beyond any doubt. He was the reigning World Champion, the World Cup winner, and had held the world number one ranking for a record-breaking period. This time, there was no question—he was China's top player and their best hope for gold.

Winning Gold for China

The men's singles event at the 2016 Rio Olympics was filled with top players from around the world. Ma Long knew he had to stay focused if he wanted to win.

In the early rounds, he defeated his opponents with ease. His combination of powerful forehands, quick footwork, and smart tactics made him unstoppable. He didn't just win—he dominated.

As he advanced through the tournament, his biggest test came in the final match. His opponent? Zhang Jike, the defending Olympic champion and his longtime rival.

The entire world was watching. Millions of fans in China stayed up late to see if Ma Long could bring home the gold. The pressure was enormous, but Ma Long reminded himself of one thing: he had prepared for this moment his entire life.

From the very first game, Ma Long played with incredible confidence. He attacked with his powerful forehand, blocked Zhang Jike's shots with precision, and moved so quickly that his opponent had no time to react.

The match was one-sided. Ma Long won 4-0, an almost unheard-of result in an Olympic final. It wasn't just a victory—it was a statement. He had completely outplayed the defending champion.

When the final point was won, Ma Long dropped his paddle and raised his arms in the air. He was now an Olympic gold medalist!

As he stood on the podium with the gold medal around his neck, Ma Long felt a wave of emotions. He thought about all the years of training, the sacrifices, and the disappointments along the way. It had all been worth it.

China's national anthem played, and Ma Long sang along, proud to represent his country on the biggest stage. At that moment, he knew he had fulfilled his childhood dream.

Making History

Winning the 2016 Olympic gold medal was a huge achievement, but Ma Long wasn't finished yet. He knew that true champions don't stop after one victory—they keep pushing forward.

After his Olympic win, many people wondered if he would retire. He had already won everything there was to win. But Ma Long wasn't ready to step away from the game.

He continued to compete at the highest level, winning more championships and setting new records. Then, in 2021, at the Tokyo Olympics, Ma Long had a chance to do something no man had ever done before—win back-to-back Olympic gold medals in men's singles.

At 32 years old, he wasn't as fast as before, and younger players like Fan Zhendong were now at their peak. But Ma Long still had the experience, the skills, and the heart of a champion.

In the Tokyo Olympic final, he faced Fan Zhendong, who had become his biggest rival. Fan was younger, stronger, and hungry for his first Olympic gold. Many believed it was finally time for a new champion.

But Ma Long had other plans.

He played with the same determination and focus that had made him a champion before. With every shot, he reminded the world why he was called "The Dragon." He defeated Fan Zhendong 4-2, becoming the first player in history to win two Olympic singles gold medals.

At that moment, there was no doubt—Ma Long was the greatest table tennis player of all time.

As he held his second gold medal, he knew that his journey had inspired young players all over the world. He had proven that with hard work, discipline, and belief in yourself, anything is possible.

And that is how Ma Long became a legend.

Chapter 6

The Grand Slam Winner

What is a Grand Slam?

In the world of table tennis, winning a single tournament is a big achievement. Winning a world championship or an Olympic gold medal is even greater. But there is one achievement that only the greatest players in history can accomplish—the Grand Slam.

A Grand Slam means winning the three biggest titles in table tennis:

1. The World Championships – The most prestigious event, held every two years.

2. The World Cup – A tournament featuring only the best players in the world.

3. The Olympic Gold Medal – The highest honor in sports, held once every four years.

Winning all three of these tournaments at least once in a career makes a player a Grand Slam champion. Only a handful of players in history had ever achieved this, including Ma Long's rival Zhang Jike and the legendary Liu Guoliang.

For years, Ma Long had come close to winning all three, but there was always one title missing. When he won the World Championships in 2015, he had two out of the three. He was already a World Cup champion, having won the title in 2012. But to complete the Grand Slam, he needed to win Olympic gold.

The 2016 Rio Olympics was his chance. If he won, he would enter the history books as one of the greatest players ever.

Completing the Ultimate Achievement

The road to the Grand Slam was not easy. Even though Ma Long had won many titles, the Olympics were different. The pressure was higher, the expectations greater, and the world was watching.

As he entered the tournament, Ma Long knew that history was on the line. He had trained for this moment for years, preparing for every possible challenge. He had already faced defeats, setbacks, and heartbreaks in past tournaments, but those only made him stronger.

From the first match in Rio, Ma Long played like a man on a mission. He didn't just win—he dominated. His footwork was fast, his shots were powerful, and his mind was focused. It was as if all his years of experience had come together perfectly at the right time.

The final match against Zhang Jike was his biggest test. Zhang was already a Grand Slam winner, and he had the experience of winning Olympic gold before. But Ma Long was unstoppable that night. He played with speed, precision, and confidence, defeating Zhang 4-0 in a one-sided final.

With that victory, Ma Long became the tenth player in history to complete the Grand Slam.

As he stood on the podium with the gold medal around his neck, the Chinese flag rising behind him, Ma Long realized that all the sacrifices, struggles, and training had led to this moment. He was now a part of table tennis history.

A Moment of Triumph

Winning the Grand Slam was a dream come true, but Ma Long was not finished. Unlike some players who slowed down after winning the biggest prizes, Ma Long kept pushing himself to new heights.

After Rio, he continued to dominate the sport. In 2017, he won the World Championships again, proving that he was still the best. In 2019, he made history by winning his third World Championship title, something very few players had ever done.

By this time, fans and experts no longer debated whether Ma Long was the best of his generation. The question had changed: Was Ma Long the greatest player of all time?

Then, in 2021, Ma Long did something that removed all doubt. At the Tokyo Olympics, he won another gold medal in men's singles, becoming the first player in history to win two Olympic singles titles.

At that moment, there was no argument left—Ma Long was the greatest table tennis player in history.

Standing on the podium once again, holding his second Olympic gold medal, Ma Long knew that his name would be remembered forever. He had not only completed the Grand Slam—he had gone beyond it.

For young players around the world, he had become a symbol of hard work, dedication, and never giving up. And that, more than anything, was his greatest achievement.

Chapter 7

A Leader on the Team

Becoming the Team Captain

Winning championships is a great achievement, but being a leader is something even more special. In 2014, Ma Long was given an important role—he became the captain of the Chinese national table tennis team.

China has always been the strongest country in table tennis. With so many talented players, the competition within the team was just as tough as international tournaments. Only the best and most respected player could become the captain.

At first, Ma Long felt the weight of responsibility. He was not just playing for himself anymore—he had to guide and inspire his teammates. He had to set an example in training, encourage younger players, and lead the team to victory in major tournaments.

His leadership was tested at the 2016 World Team Championships. China faced Japan in the final, and Ma Long, as captain, had to play the most important matches. He stepped onto the court with confidence, winning both of his matches and leading China to a 3-0 victory. With that, China secured another world title, and Ma Long proved that he was the right person to lead the team.

When he won his first Olympic gold medal later that year, his role as captain became even more meaningful. He was no longer just a champion—he was a leader, guiding the strongest table tennis team in the world.

Helping Young Players Grow

As a leader, Ma Long knew that his job was not just about winning. It was also about helping the next generation of players. He remembered how difficult it was when he was young, training hard to earn his place on the team. Now, it was his turn to support the younger players and help them succeed.

One of the rising stars during this time was Fan Zhendong. Fan was much younger than Ma Long but had incredible talent. Many people believed that he would be the next great Chinese champion. But talent alone was not enough—he needed experience, guidance, and someone to push him to be better.

Ma Long became that person. He trained with Fan, giving him advice and helping him improve his mental game. They often faced each other in big matches, with Ma Long winning most of the time. But instead of feeling discouraged, Fan kept learning from those battles.

Outside of tournaments, Ma Long also helped other young players, like Lin Gaoyuan and Liang Jingkun. He taught them how to stay calm under pressure, how to handle tough losses, and how to keep improving even after winning. He showed them that being great was not just about talent—it was about hard work, discipline, and never giving up.

Because of Ma Long's leadership, the Chinese team remained the strongest in the world. Even as new generations of players arrived, the team continued to dominate international tournaments.

Leading China to More Victories

Under Ma Long's leadership, China won many major team tournaments, including:

- The World Team Championships (2016, 2018, 2022)
- The Olympic Team Gold Medal (2016, 2021)

One of the most memorable moments came at the 2021 Tokyo Olympics. Ma Long, at 32 years old, was no longer the youngest player on the team. Many thought this might be his last Olympics. But as captain, he still played an important role.

In the team final against Germany, Ma Long stepped up once again. He won his match with powerful attacks and smart tactics, helping China secure another gold medal. With that victory, China had won every

Olympic men's team event since 2008, proving their continued dominance.

As the team celebrated, younger players looked at Ma Long with admiration. He had led them to victory once again, showing them what it meant to be a true champion.

Even as he grew older, Ma Long remained a key figure in the team. His experience, leadership, and passion for table tennis kept China at the top.

A great player wins titles, but a great leader builds a legacy. And that is exactly what Ma Long had done.

Chapter 8

Challenges and Comebacks

Fighting Through Injuries

Being a champion isn't just about winning—it's also about overcoming challenges. Ma Long was one of the greatest table tennis players in history, but even he faced tough moments. One of his biggest struggles was dealing with injuries.

For many years, Ma Long had played at the highest level, competing in tournaments all over the world. His fast movements and powerful shots put a lot of stress on his body. By 2018, his knees started giving him trouble. The pain was sharp, especially when he moved quickly or bent his legs for low shots.

Doctors told him that he needed time to rest. But resting meant missing tournaments, and Ma Long didn't want to stop playing. He tried to push through the pain, but it only made things worse. In 2019, the injury became so serious that he had to take a break from table tennis.

For months, he focused on recovery. He worked with doctors, did special exercises, and followed strict treatments. It was not easy. Watching other players compete while he was stuck on the sidelines was frustrating. Some people even thought his career might be over.

But Ma Long refused to give up. He knew that if he wanted to return, he had to be patient and let his body heal properly. He told himself, "I have come too far to stop now."

Overcoming Doubts

While recovering, Ma Long faced something even harder than physical pain—doubt.

He had been the best player in the world for many years, but now, younger players like Fan Zhendong and Lin Gaoyuan were rising fast. They were strong, hungry for victory, and eager to take his place at the top.

People began asking:

- "Is Ma Long too old?"
- "Can he still compete with younger players?"
- "Will he ever be the same again?"

These questions were everywhere. Even Ma Long wondered if he could return to his best form. Doubt is one of the hardest battles an athlete can face.

But instead of letting doubt defeat him, Ma Long used it as motivation. He reminded himself why he started playing table tennis in the first place—not for titles or trophies, but for the love of the game.

So, he worked harder than ever. Every day, he trained, even when his knees hurt. Every night, he watched his old matches, studying his movements and finding ways to improve. He refused to believe that his time was over.

Returning Stronger

After months of recovery, Ma Long finally returned to competition in late 2019. But he didn't just come back—he came back stronger than ever.

In the 2019 World Table Tennis Championships, many people thought he might struggle. But Ma Long shocked the world by winning the title, defeating Fan Zhendong in the final. With this victory, he became the first player to win three consecutive World Championships (2015, 2017, and 2019).

It was an incredible comeback. He had gone from injury and doubt to standing at the top once again.

Then, in 2021, he faced his biggest challenge yet—the Tokyo Olympics. Now 32 years old, Ma Long was no longer the fastest or strongest player. Fan Zhendong had taken the world's number one ranking, and many believed it was time for a new champion.

But Ma Long had experience, skill, and the heart of a true fighter. In the Olympic final, he played against Fan Zhendong, the younger star who had trained under him for years. The match was intense, but Ma Long proved why he was the greatest, winning 4-2 and securing his second Olympic gold medal in men's singles.

With this victory, he became the only man in history to win two Olympic singles gold medals.

As he held his medal, Ma Long felt proud—not just because he had won, but because he had overcome the toughest challenges of his career.

His journey was proof that true champions don't just win when things are easy. They fight through pain, push past doubt, and come back even stronger.

And that is exactly what Ma Long did.

Chapter 9

More Than a Champion

Inspiring the Next Generation

Ma Long's success in table tennis made him one of the greatest players of all time. But his impact went beyond winning matches and breaking records. He inspired millions of young players who dreamed of following in his footsteps.

All over China, kids practiced their forehand and backhand, trying to copy Ma Long's powerful shots. Some even watched his matches over and over again, studying how he moved and how he stayed calm under pressure. To them, Ma Long wasn't just a champion—he was a hero.

One of those young players was Fan Zhendong, who would later become one of Ma Long's biggest rivals. As a child, Fan looked up to Ma Long, admiring his work ethic and discipline. Years later, he would train with him, learning from the very person he once idolized.

But Ma Long didn't just inspire kids in China—his influence spread across the world. From Europe to the United States, young players watched him with awe, hoping to one day play like him. Many even called him their role model, not just because of his skills but because of his attitude—humble, hardworking, and never giving up.

Even after reaching the top, Ma Long always took time to encourage young athletes. He often visited training centers, spoke to junior players, and shared his experiences. He wanted them to know that success wasn't about talent alone—it was about dedication, patience, and believing in yourself.

Sportsmanship and Respect

Winning was important to Ma Long, but respecting his opponents was just as important. Throughout his career, he showed great sportsmanship, whether he won or lost.

In table tennis, matches can get intense. Players fight for every point, and emotions run high. But Ma Long never disrespected his opponents. If he won, he stayed humble. If he lost, he accepted defeat with grace, congratulating the winner.

One of the best examples of his sportsmanship came at the 2017 World Table Tennis Championships. After winning a hard-fought final against Fan Zhendong, instead of celebrating wildly, Ma Long walked over and hugged his young opponent. He knew how hard Fan had trained and respected his effort. That simple gesture showed the world what kind of person he was—not just a great champion, but also a great sportsman.

His respect for the game extended beyond his matches. He always listened to his coaches, supported his teammates, and played by the rules. He showed that being a true champion wasn't just about skill—it was about honor, discipline, and respect.

Because of this, Ma Long earned the admiration of fans, players, and even his rivals. He became not only the face of Chinese table tennis but also an ambassador for the sport worldwide.

Giving Back to the Sport

Ma Long never forgot where he came from. He remembered being a young boy, practicing for hours every day, hoping to one day wear the Chinese team jersey. Now that he had achieved his dreams, he wanted to give back to the sport that had given him so much.

Over the years, Ma Long worked to promote table tennis around the world. He took part in charity events, training camps, and special coaching sessions for young players. He used his fame to bring more attention to the sport, encouraging more kids to pick up a paddle and start playing.

Even as he got older and neared the end of his career, he continued to mentor the younger generation. He helped train future stars like Wang Chuqin, sharing his knowledge and experience. He wanted to make sure that even after he retired, China would remain the strongest table tennis nation.

Many believed that after Ma Long stopped competing, he would become a coach or leader in Chinese table tennis, helping shape the next generation of champions. His passion for the sport never faded, and he remained dedicated to its growth.

For Ma Long, table tennis was never just a game. It was his life, his passion, and his way of inspiring others.

He had won every major title, broken records, and made history. But his greatest achievement was not just what he did on the table—it was the way he inspired the world, proving that with hard work, respect, and a true love for the game, anything is possible.

Chapter 10

The Legend Lives On

Breaking Records

Ma Long didn't just win tournaments—he rewrote the history books. Throughout his career, he set records that no one had ever achieved before. Some of these records may stand for decades, proving just how special he was.

Here are some of his most incredible achievements:

- Two Olympic gold medals in men's singles (2016, 2021) – The first male table tennis player ever to do this.

- Four Olympic gold medals overall – Two in singles and two in team events.

- Three consecutive World Championship titles (2015, 2017, 2019) – A record in modern table tennis.

- Most ITTF World Tour titles in history – Winning more international tournaments than any other player.

- Table Tennis Grand Slam winner – Holding Olympic, World Championship, and World Cup titles at the same time.

Winning once is hard. Winning again and again, year after year, is even harder. But Ma Long did it because of his hard work, determination, and love for the sport.

Even as he grew older and younger stars rose in the rankings, Ma Long never backed down. Every match he played was proof of his endless dedication to excellence.

What Makes Ma Long Special?

Many great players have come and gone, but Ma Long was different. What made him stand above the rest?

First, his work ethic. He trained harder than anyone else. Even after winning everything, he still pushed himself to improve. He never settled for being "good enough." He always wanted to be better than yesterday.

Second, his mental strength. Table tennis moves at lightning speed. A single mistake can change the entire match. But Ma Long stayed calm under pressure. He never panicked, no matter how tough things got. That's why he won so many big matches, even against younger, faster opponents.

Third, his respect for the game. He never bragged or looked down on others. He treated every opponent with honor. Win or lose, he always showed sportsmanship and humility.

And finally, his leadership. He wasn't just a great player—he was a captain, a mentor, and an inspiration to millions. He helped young players grow, making sure that China's table tennis dominance would continue for years to come.

Ma Long was more than just a champion. He was a role model, a legend, and a symbol of greatness.

His Legacy in Table Tennis

Every sport has legends—people whose names will be remembered forever. In table tennis, one of those names will always be Ma Long.

His influence can be seen in the young players who grew up watching him. Many of today's stars, like Fan Zhendong and Wang Chuqin, were inspired by his playing style. They learned from his matches, trained with him, and are now carrying on his legacy.

His records will be studied by future players, and his matches will be replayed for years to come. Kids in training halls all over the world will continue to dream of being "the next Ma Long."

Even if one day he steps away from professional play, his impact on table tennis will never fade. He will always be known as one of the greatest to ever pick up a paddle.

Ma Long's story is about more than just table tennis. It's a story of hard work, resilience, and never giving up. It's about believing in yourself, even when others doubt you. It's about chasing your dreams and inspiring others along the way.

No matter what sport you love, or what dreams you have, Ma Long's journey teaches us something important—greatness is not given, it is earned.

And Ma Long earned it, every step of the way.

We hope you enjoyed reading about Ma Long's incredible journey. If you loved this book, please **leave a positive review on Amazon**! Your support helps us create more amazing books for readers like you.

Also, be sure to check out more of our books by searching for **"Dale J. Gibson" on Amazon**. There are many more exciting stories waiting for you!

Thank you, and keep chasing your dreams—just like Ma Long!

Fun Facts, Glossary and Fun Quiz

Fun Facts About Ma Long

1. **Nicknamed "The Dragon"** – Ma Long's nickname in Chinese, "马龙" (Mǎ Lóng), means "Horse Dragon." His fierce playing style earned him the title "The Dragon" in table tennis.

2. **Youngest World Champion in Team Event** – Ma Long was only **17 years old** when he won his first World Championship gold medal as part of China's team in **2006**!

3. **First Male Player to Win Two Olympic Singles Golds** – Ma Long made history by winning gold in men's singles at both the **2016 Rio Olympics** and **2021 Tokyo Olympics**.

4. **Longest Reigning World No. 1** – Ma Long held the **world No. 1 ranking** for **64 months in total**, the longest in table tennis history!

5. **Table Tennis Grand Slam Winner** – He is one of the few players in history to win an **Olympic gold, World Championship, and World Cup**, completing the Grand Slam in **2016**.

6. **Once Won 35 Matches in a Row** – In the **ITTF World Tour**, Ma Long won an incredible **35 consecutive matches**, showing his dominance over the competition.

7. **Loves Basketball** – Outside of table tennis, Ma Long enjoys watching and playing **basketball**. He has said that he admires NBA players for their athleticism and mindset.

8. **A Team Captain and a Mentor** – Ma Long was chosen as the **captain of the Chinese national team**, leading and guiding younger players like Fan Zhendong and Wang Chuqin.

9. **Overcame Injuries and Doubts** – Despite struggling with knee injuries later in his career, he made a **strong comeback** to win gold at the **Tokyo 2021 Olympics**.

10. **One of the Most Respected Players in Table Tennis** – Not only is he known for his skill, but also for his **sportsmanship and respect** toward his opponents, making him a true role model for young athletes.

Glossary

1. **Backhand** – A stroke in table tennis where the back of the hand faces the opponent while hitting the ball.

2. **Forehand** – A stroke where the palm of the hand faces the opponent while hitting the ball.

3. **Grand Slam** – In table tennis, winning the **Olympics, World Championships, and World Cup** in a career.

4. **ITTF** – Stands for **International Table Tennis Federation**, the organization that oversees table tennis worldwide.

5. **Olympic Games** – A global sports competition held every four years where athletes compete for gold, silver, and bronze medals.

6. **Spin** – When a player hits the ball in a way that makes it rotate quickly, changing how it moves when it bounces.

7. **Sportsmanship** – Showing respect, fairness, and good behavior in sports, whether you win or lose.

8. **Topspin** – A type of spin that makes the ball dip down quickly after bouncing.

9. **World Ranking** – A system used to rank table tennis players based on their performance in international tournaments.

10. **World Championships** – One of the biggest table tennis tournaments, held every two years, where the best players compete for the title.

Quiz: How Well Do You Know Ma Long?

1. What is Ma Long's nickname?

    a) The Phoenix

    b) The Dragon

    c) The Tiger

    d) The King

2. How many Olympic gold medals has Ma Long won in singles?

    a) 1

    b) 2

    c) 3

    d) 4

3. What year did Ma Long win his first Olympic singles gold medal?

    a) 2012

    b) 2016

    c) 2020

    d) 2024

4. How long was Ma Long ranked world No. 1 in total?

    a) 30 months

    b) 40 months

    c) 50 months

    d) 64 months

5. What is the name of the major organization that oversees table tennis worldwide?

   a) ITTF

   b) FIFA

   c) NBA

   d) IOC

6. What is a Grand Slam in table tennis?

   a) Winning three ITTF World Tour events

   b) Winning an Olympic gold, World Championship, and World Cup

   c) Winning a national championship

   d) Winning ten matches in a row

7. Who is one of Ma Long's biggest rivals in table tennis?

   a) Michael Jordan

   b) Roger Federer

   c) Fan Zhendong

   d) Cristiano Ronaldo

8. What sport does Ma Long enjoy watching besides table tennis?

   a) Soccer

   b) Basketball

   c) Tennis

   d) Baseball

9. What kind of spin makes the ball dip down quickly after bouncing?

   a) Backspin

   b) Sidespin

   c) No spin

   d) Topspin

10. What quality is Ma Long especially known for, besides his skills?

    a) Speed

    b) Sportsmanship

    c) Loud celebrations

    d) Playing with a wooden paddle

Quiz Answers

1. **b) The Dragon**
2. **b) 2**
3. **b) 2016**
4. **d) 64 months**
5. **a) ITTF**
6. **b) Winning an Olympic gold, World Championship, and World Cup**
7. **c) Fan Zhendong**
8. **b) Basketball**
9. **d) Topspin**
10. **b) Sportsmanship**

Made in the USA
Monee, IL
25 May 2025